THE
LEADERSHIP GARDEN®
GUIDEBOOK

Cultivating organic experiences, actions, and results
that empower you and those around you.

By Debra J. Slover

LEADER
GARDEN
PRESS

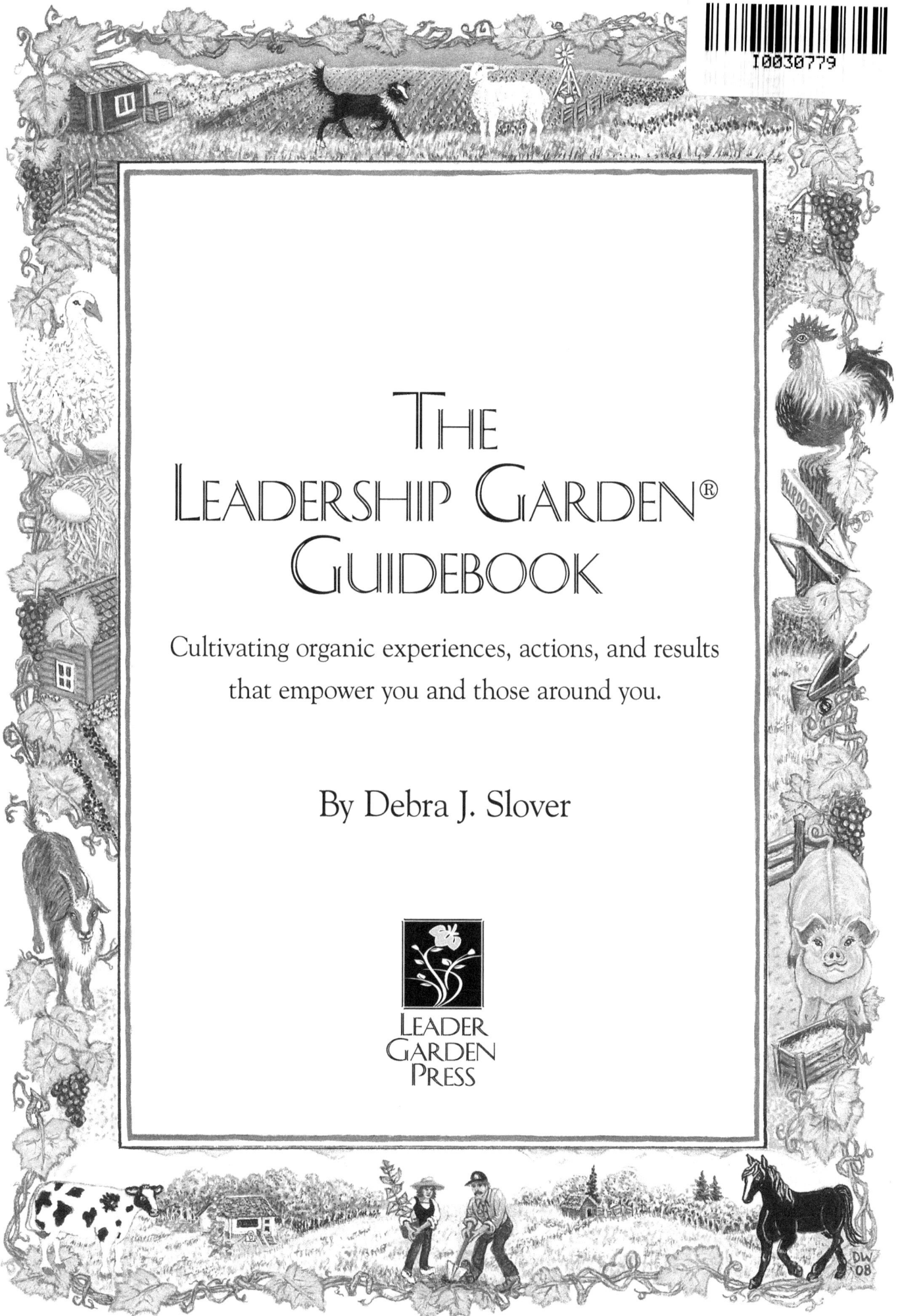

CONTENTS

LEADERSHIP GARDEN® LEGACY

Every person is a unique seed in the world's garden.
Each seed grows a leader from which greatness can blossom.
Imagine the future of our planet if we nurture
each leader to sprout greatness.
—Debra J. Slover

INTRODUCTION

True leadership is not a title, position, or job. It's a way of life that expresses your imagination, purpose, and spirit. What brings these qualities to life is unique in everyone.

The Leadership Garden Guidebook presents an organic view of leadership, using a garden metaphor to help you *tap* into your imagination, dreams and spirit, to make leadership accessible to everyone.

All plants have a primary shoot called the leader, which eventually blooms. Like plants, you have a leader waiting to blossom.

This Guidebook is an extraction of the lessons and an expansion of the exercises outlined in the primer for Leadership Gardens—*U.N.I.Q.U.E.: Growing the Leader Within.* In this book, when Hugh, the lost sheep, wanders onto the Leadership Farm he symbolizes the heart, mind, and spirit in each of you. Hugh learns how to grow his Leadership Garden

and takes the U.N.I.Q.U.E. Tour with a Border collie named Annabelle, who stands for the favor, grace, and beauty of life.

Though the main character and fable are symbolic of being lost at times in the complexity of life, the lessons are real. They are designed to ignite your passion, focus your energy, and claim your power to make the difference you truly desire.

The acronym, U.N.I.Q.U.E. is the Understanding, Nurturing, Inventive, Quality, Unstoppable, Expression of leadership that is essential to grow and sprout your Leadership Garden Legacy.

In this Guidebook, you'll learn how to connect your heart, mind, and spirit in a new way. You'll plant new seeds, uproot weeds, and learn leader-friendly gardening practices that empower you and those around you to thrive.

Each lesson outlines the principles or practices for growing a thriving Leadership Garden and concludes with exercises.

As the natural steward of your Leadership Garden, you become the trusted guide who directs your life and creates the space for true empowerment to take place. You'll find it's a delicate balance to prevent judgmental behavior, gossip, and blame from seeping into this pristine place and rendering you a victim of your life circumstances. This Guidebook affords you the opportunity to look at *what* you do, *how* you do it, and *why* you do it, so you can begin to choose and write your thriving Leadership Garden Legacy.

It is important to remember that your greatness sprouts, not in spite of your imperfections, but from the wisdom you gain as you improve upon them. By taking this journey, you will increase your capacity to empower yourself and engage those around you and write your own Leadership Garden Legacy story.

So let's begin on your journey.

Please note: The title of the Guidebook lessons remain the same as the chapter titles of the Leadership Garden primer *U.N.I.Q.U.E.: Growing the Leader Within* book and audio book, as well as the fall release of our children's book: *U.N.I.Q.U.E. KIDS: Growing My Leadership Garden* (for 8- to 12-year-olds). This is done to help you use the various Leadership Garden empowerment tools conveniently.

Part One

Welcome to the Leadership Farm

Notes

A weed takes little effort to survive in a garden, yet the choice to grow a thriving garden requires the synergy of the heart, mind, and spirit with purpose and aim.
—Debra J. Slover

LESSON 1
LEADERSHIP GARDEN®

Life begins as a seed that grows roots and a leader that has the potential to sprout personal greatness. Roots grow from your family and your own life experiences. In gardening, the leader is the stem—the primary shoot of a plant that will eventually produce flowers or fruits. Your leader is your mind, heart, and spirit. Like plants, each person is a leader waiting to sprout. Once it has blossomed, the leader inside you re-sows the seeds of greatness and distributes them in the gardens of others.

Your body is the soil of your Leadership Garden, where the heart, mind, and spirit grow. The mind creates thoughts; the logic and reasoning you use to interpret the world. Your heart elicits physical responses to feelings, emotions, and passion. Your spirit nurtures the values, conscience, attitudes, and principles that provoke your thoughts, actions, and purpose.

The root of the word "leadership" is lead, which means to guide and direct. Your leader guides and directs your life and the actions you take that convey your leadership. To grow a Leadership Garden, the heart, mind, and spirit connect to plant and nurture the seeds of your best purpose and aim. Without purpose and aim, weeds can overrun your life and your Leadership Garden will be smothered and die.

In Leadership Gardens, two different conditions affect the growth of a leader. A *survival condition* allows the growth of weeds, tenacious plants with deep taproots. These weeds diminish personal power and enable gossip, blame, and victimization. A *thriving condition* promotes vigorous, flourishing, and expansive growth, rooted in a strong mesh-like network of understanding and nurturing the inventive quality of an unstoppable expression of leadership.

You cannot always control the circumstances of your life, but you can always choose how you respond to them. When you want your garden to thrive, rather than be smothered by weeds, you choose to pull your weeds and plant new seeds that empower you.

A thriving Leadership Garden relies upon the *empowerment* and *engagement* of your unique *legacy*. In this context, empowerment means to endow with ability; engagement means to put into action; and a legacy is the way of thinking and behaving handed down from your ancestors and created by life experiences. The truth is, you already empower and engage your leadership legacy. But is it the one you truly desire?

EXERCISE 1: EMPOWER AND ENGAGE

A) Make a list of *at least* three things that you don't currently have and want. It could be something you want to do, obtain, or experience as a feeling that relates to any area of your life.

What I Want in My Life:

_____

_____

_____

_____

_____

_____

_____

_____

_____

_____

_____

_____

_____

_____

_____

_____

_____

_____

_____

_____

_____

_____

_____

_____

B) Make a list of *at least* three things that you currently have that you don't want. Again, it could be something you do, have, or experience as a feeling that relates to any area of your life.

What I Don't Want in My Life:

_____

_____

_____

_____

_____

_____

_____

_____

_____

_____

_____

_____

_____

_____

_____

_____

_____

_____

_____

_____

_____

_____

_____

_____

_____

_____

_____

_____

_____

C) Describe below a difficult relationship or situation where you used *survival leadership* or walked away:

_____

_____

_____

_____

_____

_____

_____

State your thoughts regarding that relationship or situation. Below are some examples to get you started. Use only those that apply to you:

I'm too _____

If only _____

They don't _____

I can't _____

They are _____

I should _____

They shouldn't _____

It's not _____

_____

_____

_____

_____

_____

_____

_____

_____

_____

Ask yourself if these statements empower a thriving leadership condition. Write yes or no beside each statement. Cross out the "no" statements and circle the "yes" statements to use as a reminder for the next lesson.

D) Describe below a difficult relationship or situation where you used *thriving leadership* and turned it around:

_____

_____

_____

_____

_____

State your thoughts regarding that relationship or situation. Below are some examples to get you started. Use only those that apply to you:

I did _____

I felt _____

I thought _____

I can _____

They are _____

I should _____

They can _____

It is _____

_____

_____

_____

_____

_____

Ask yourself if these statements empower a thriving leadership condition. Write yes or no beside each statement. Cross out the "no" statements and circle the "yes" statements to use as a reminder for the next lesson.

Please note: As you continue through the rest of the exercises, feel free to go back to the first two pages of this exercise and add to the list of what you want or don't want in your life.

Reality germinates from the seeds of early life experience.
If those seeds don't give you power, you can choose to
cultivate and replant a new Leadership Garden.
—Debra J. Slover

Lesson 2
Planting a Leadership Garden

You create your reality by the seeds you plant and nurture in your Leadership Garden. In Chapter One, we discussed how the condition of your garden determines how your leader grows. Now we'll explore how that condition evolves from your view of reality.

Your unique genetic make-up influences how you interpret your environment, and that interpretation wires your brain, gives you the ability to function in the world, and creates your reality. It's human nature to seek what is pleasant and to avoid the unpleasant. You have a natural need to express yourself, search for meaning in life, and protect yourself from danger and threats. Pulling weeds enables you to thrive and re-sow seeds that will grant you the ability to experience your greatness—the essence of who you are.

To learn how to pull your weeds, let's look at the basic "empowerment" principle of Leadership Gardens, beginning with your mind. The elaborate mapping of the brain helps you learn from, and respond to, both pleasant and unpleasant life events.

Scientists previously thought the brain was hard-wired by genetics and early life experiences. Recently, scientists studying the brain discovered that we have the ability to rewire our brain in order to learn new things and create new experiences. In other words, our wiring is not fixed.

To help understand this, we'll look at the brain's wiring process. It begins with a stimulus (seed) that comes into your body through one or more of your senses. You either notice or ignore the stimulus. If noticed, the stimulus is sent to your short-term memory. From there, you interpret and learn what is meaningful or useful and store it in one of your two long-term memory compartments for later retrieval.

Your explicit (conscious) memory stores the biographical events of your life, along with words, ideas, and concepts. Your implicit (nonconscious) memory stores procedural skills—like riding a bike or driving a car—and emotional conditioning from past events. (**Note:** In my literature research, I found that neuroscientists use the term, "nonconscious," and psychologists use the term, "subconscious," to refer to the implicit memory. Regardless of the term, we are conscious but not aware. For simplicity, I'll use the commonly used term, "unconscious.")

When you receive a new stimulus, an impulse is sent to the heart and other organs that evoke feelings—pleasant, unpleasant, or neutral. The brain then calls up an emotional reaction that tells you how to respond to the stimuli. This all takes place simultaneously through nerve cells that fire neurotransmitters—chemical substances—across a synapse to other parts of your brain and body. Consequently, you learn by paying attention to your *feelings* and respond with both *conscious thought* and *automatic emotional conditioning*. This response completes the wiring process that creates your view of reality and the condition of your Leadership Garden.

Intuition, often referred to as our sixth sense, is not connected to the sensory organs, *per se*, but it plays a key role in leadership, especially when it connects to your values, conscience, and purpose. Intuition is like a "gut feeling" or insight; there may not be any rational or tangible evidence to support or explain it, but you feel it as something real. If this feeling empowers you, pay attention; if not, you should ignore it.

Feelings and emotions also play a key role in the empowerment principle. Feelings and emotions are often thought of as interchangeable and heart-centered, not mind-centered. Feelings are your body's response to emotions. Your emotions are evaluated and interpreted in the brain and reside in your long-term memory.

There is also a part of the brain called the amygdala, often referred to as the "reptilian" or "primal brain" that resides outside of our long-term memory, yet plays an important role in the stimulus input and response output of the brain's wiring. The amygdala is the survival mechanism in all animal species. Its function is arousal and it controls autonomic responses associated with fear or anxiety, and is known to cause a *fight, flee,* or *freeze* response to danger.

Prolonged triggering of this mechanism in humans becomes part of the automatic emotional conditioning of the long-term memory compartment, even when life-threatening situations do not exist and it is fueled by hate and greed. I mention it here to make note that constant fear and anxiety wreak havoc on your ability to discern *real* from *imagined* threats in an attempt to protect the identity of the ego that you have already developed.

Stored in your long-term memory compartments are what psychologist's term, "corrective emotional experiences," (CEE's) for individuals, and, "collective emotional experiences," for groups. CEE's for groups are large-scale societal/historical events such as Pearl Harbor, September 11th, Hurricane Katrina, and the election of Barack Obama.

Whether in a group or as individual events, I'll call these experiences, "source events." Simply put, source events are experiences you cannot change. No matter how old you are when a source event occurs, it leaves its mark in your long-term memory compartments. Though the response you have may be similar to others, because of your unique wiring, no two people have the same exact emotional response to any one event.

Source events are neutral and have no power. The power lies in how your long-term memory is wired. Your emotional conditioning evokes an automatic reaction and then a response. Present and past events have no actual association, but the automatic reaction and response, triggered by a stimulus or fear, may be the same. When the source event is retrieved by your conscious memory, it may cause you to relive an unpleasant experience with thoughts such as, *If only . . . I should have . . . Why did . . .* etc. These thoughts lead to regret, guilt, and dissatisfaction, and reinforce the smothering survival condition of your Leadership Garden.

Since you now know that you have the ability to rewire certain parts of your brain, here is the key to empowerment: CHOICE. Choice gives you the ability to:

- discern imagined threats triggered by fear from physical danger that is real
- choose your response to automatic emotional conditioning
- accept the things you cannot change

You possess this power of choice, the empowerment key to your Leadership Garden. Not all source events are dramatic or unpleasant; even pleasant ones leave their mark in your long-term memory. Each time you choose to focus on the pleasant events of your life, and not let the unpleasant ones dictate your response in a negative manner, you begin to rewire your brain, create a new reality, and rewrite your Leadership Garden Legacy story.

NOTES

_____

_____

_____

_____

_____

_____

_____

_____

_____

_____

_____

_____

_____

_____

_____

_____

_____

_____

_____

EXERCISE 2: REALITY CHECK

Write down three recent experiences (or situations) that evoked a strong emotional reaction and go through this three-step process:

- Identify your physical sensation (feelings), your instant emotional reaction, and your instant thought to each experience.
- Identify whether the emotional response(s) and the action(s) you took was a smothering weed or blossoming seed in your garden.
- See if there was a source event connected to each incident.

Experience/situation 1:_____

_____

_____

_____

- Physical sensation: _____
- Emotional reaction: _____
- Instant thought: _____

_____

_____

- Did you stop here to think and assess your emotional reaction and choose a new emotional response?   □ Yes   □ No
- What was the action you took? _____

_____

_____

_____

- Was the response and action you took a weed or an empowering seed? Explain:

_____

- Source event?_____

_____

_____

15

Experience/situation 2: _____

_____

_____

- Physical sensation: _____
- Emotional reaction: _____
- Instant thought: _____
- Did you stop here to think and assess your emotional reaction and choose a new emotional response?   □ Yes   □ No
- What was the action you took? _____
- Was the response and action you took a weed or an empowering seed? Explain:

  _____
- Source event? _____

  _____

  _____

Experience/situation 3: _____

_____

_____

- Physical sensation: _____
- Emotional reaction: _____
- Instant thought: _____
- Did you stop here to think and assess your emotional reaction and choose a new emotional response?   □ Yes   □ No
- What was the action you took? _____
- Was the response and action you took a weed or an empowering seed? Explain:

  _____
- Source event? _____

  _____

  _____

Now go back to the first exercise and see if any of the *If only . . . I should . . . They don't . . . etc.* statements you created are related to a source event that you can now choose to accept to empower yourself.

Take a moment to free write with these questions in mind:

- Are there any insights you have about yourself by looking at these three experiences/situations using the Reality Check framework?
- Are there any similarities or patterns?

_____

_____

_____

_____

_____

_____

_____

_____

Also make note of any questions you have at this point that you would like to have answered. By listing your questions, your answers may surface from within you as you proceed with the rest of the Guidebook Lessons and Exercises. If you don't have your answers by the time you complete your Guidebook, you can go to our web site and pose your questions for a personal response at: *www.leadershipgardenlegacy.com*

_____

_____

_____

_____

_____

_____

_____

NOTES

_____
_____
_____
_____
_____
_____
_____
_____
_____
_____
_____
_____
_____
_____
_____
_____
_____
_____
_____
_____
_____
_____
_____
_____
_____
_____
_____

PART TWO

THE U.N.I.Q.U.E. TOUR BEGINS

Before you proceed—list your top *three* concerns in the following four categories:

Personal:

_____

_____

_____

Family:

_____

_____

_____

Community:

_____

_____

_____

Global:

_____

_____

_____

You will use these concerns to reflect back and assess:

1. Are they worthy of your time and energy?
2. Do they empower you to make the difference you desire with your unique purpose and aim?

To *think global* and *act local* is the gateway to your thriving Leadership Garden.

   Journey on!

Like beauty is in the eye of the beholder, thought is in the mind,
love is in the heart, and truth is in the spirit of a leader.
—Debra J. Slover

Love binds you with others and is at the heart of all authentic leadership. When leadership is only thought of in terms of leading others to make things happen, your personal leadership power diminishes. Leadership without love is simply control of another, and that is not what true leadership is about.

On the U.N.I.Q.U.E. Tour, you will learn how to blend your heart, mind, and spirit together, and unearth your unique ability to empower and connect well with others. You'll discover the honor and privilege of leadership, and how it warms your heart and lifts your spirit when used in service of another's greatness. A leader who thrives connects all three to see the favor, grace, and beauty of being a *human* leader. What follows is a summary of your U.N.I.Q.U.E. Tour lessons:

- *Understanding Field:* you learn how to balance, blend, and expand your **four leader behaviors.**
- *Nurturing Meadow:* you learn the **leader-friendly gardening practices** that keep your garden thriving.
- *Inventive Roost:* you invent your **unique purpose and aim** and hatch new ways of being.
- *Quality Yard:* you discover the **golden egg of leadership** and the **attributes** that are essential to all thriving Leadership Gardens.
- *Unstoppable Pasture:* you learn about the **circle of commitment** and how to overcome the **commitment paradox** to become unstoppable with your purpose and aim.
- *Expression Pen* you learn how to **communicate authentically** your unique purpose and aim.

NOTES

You are the natural cultivator of your Leadership Garden
to balance, blend, and expand your behaviors to thrive.
—Debra J. Slover

LESSON 3
UNDERSTANDING FIELD

The next principle of a Leadership Garden is the cultivation of the behavior that will sprout your leader. Behavior indicates how you act, what you do, and who you think you are. When you cultivate your Leadership Garden, you fertilize four specific leader behaviors: *visualize, organize, harmonize, and energize.* The condition of your garden, your view of reality, and the survival or thriving tendencies of each behavior determines how your garden grows. Tendencies, defined in this context, are ways of behaving that take you in a certain direction and always produce the same result. Conscious and unconscious emotional conditioning frames your survival or thriving behavior tendencies.

Your dreams, aspirations, career goals, and/or relationships can become thwarted when you are unaware of the survival behavior tendencies you've established, and the labels that you have placed on yourself.

Behaviors that encumber you I'll call, "spirit blockers." They seem fixed and unchangeable, but I have found that no behavior is fixed. Spirit blockers usually crop up when you are operating in a survival condition, allowing the repetition of a behavior that doesn't empower you. Thriving leaders take responsibility for everything that grows in their gardens, even weed-like survival behaviors.

So how do you alter your behavior and thrive? First, you need to let go of the notion that a particular behavior is fixed or is your true self. Then you look at the behaviors that block your leader spirit from thriving—this is where courage and choice come into play. It is not always easy to be responsible for your behavior in a survival condition, but when you are committed to thrive, the cultivation process becomes natural.

Synergy is important in leadership and in gardening. Gardeners use the term synergy to define three or more units, common characteristics, colors, or textures of flowers or plants that create a unique garden design. The individual units alone are not a complete design, but when combined with others, they create an artistic whole that provides rhythm and balance. In Leadership Gardens, the synergy of the four behaviors gives you the design that makes your ideals, goals, and dreams come true.

Please note: Pause and go to page 29 to complete the Leader Balance Inventory. Then follow the instructions to complete your Leader Balance Wheel on page 31. Resume reading when you have completed both.

The Leader Balance Wheel is a tool to help you cultivate, grow, and expand your Leadership Garden. Your Balance Wheel is always changing and most likely does not show your four behaviors equally balanced. No one behavior is better than the other, and should not be used to stereotype yourself or others. Your highest score shows you how you view the world most often. Your second highest score shows you how you accomplish tasks most often.

Now that you are aware of the unique synergy of your leader behavior, you will notice that *visualize, organize, harmonize, and energize* all denote action. You need all four to grow a strong and healthy Leadership Garden. When you understand the survival and thriving tendencies of each behavior, and how to cultivate them, your garden will blossom.

A thriving leader guides or directs at the appropriate times. Visualizing and organizing are *direction-oriented* behaviors, harmonizing and energizing are *guidance-oriented* behaviors. On the next page are the ***thriving tendencies*** of each behavior:

- *Visualize* is abstract in nature and grows thoughts, inspiration, imagination, ideas, and vision for purpose and aim.
- *Organize* is concrete in nature and grows methodology, order, and structure to fulfill goals.
- *Harmonize* is symbolic in nature and grows attunement, coordination, unity, and peace with inner self and others.
- *Energize* is literal in nature and grows play, vitality, strength, and joy for the adventure of life.

The survival tendencies of each behavior can be a source of dissatisfaction when working with others. When you are under stress, they tend to surface as emotional reactions. It is then that they act like weeds and uproot the full potential of your thriving behavior. Below are the **survival tendencies** of each behavior:

- *Visualize* grows dissatisfaction, self-centeredness, skepticism, difficulty, irritation, frustration, and feelings of being overwhelmed.
- *Organize* grows demands, criticism, self-righteousness, insensitivity, negativity, and control.
- *Harmonize* grows impracticality, defensiveness, drama, sensitivity, disagreeableness, distrust, and the need to withdraw.
- *Energize* grows reactivity, impatience, inconsideration, frustration, disruptiveness, anger, cynicism, and impulsiveness.

When looking at your Balance Wheel, you will notice that all of these behaviors are growing to some degree. When purpose and aim guide your leader and direct your behavior, you will nurture, blend, and balance all four behaviors to thrive and unearth the true leader within. You will learn to work well with others, pull weeds, and remove spirit blockers in your own garden and support others to do the same.

A key element of all behavior is emotion. A prolonged emotional state often turns into a mood that affects your behavior and those around you. When a leader becomes moody, rigid, or stagnant, progress stops, emotions run high, and what is possible to achieve as an individual, or in a group is compromised. Emotional conditioning also plays a key role in these leader behaviors. The good news and bad news is that your emotions and moods are contagious and displayed in your behavior.

Now that you've looked at the thriving and survival tendencies of each behavior, let's look at how these behaviors can **challenge** leaders who work to make their goals and dreams a reality:

- *Visualize*—the challenge is to have ideas, dreams, and visions that make sense to others, and become a reality. Staying on task or completing a project before beginning a new one can result in repeated failure and leaves others confused, overwhelmed, diminished, and annoyed.
- *Organize*—the challenge is to expand your thinking beyond the facts that pose as reality. When you discount ideas that can't be proven, you exclude new ideas and will stifle positive personal interaction and the creativity of others.
- *Harmonize*—the challenge is to not take the words and actions of others personally. When facing disagreement, always speak out or stand up for ideas that can make a valuable contribution.
- *Energize*—the challenge is to play inside conventional structures and rules. Impatience with process, and the desire to avoid routine and boredom, can have a negative impact on a group's process.

People will only take so much direction from you before their leader balance and creativity becomes compromised. When you allow others to be themselves, without trying to fix or change them, and focus on their positive behaviors, extraordinary results show up. If that's not happening, you know it's time to cultivate and weed your garden.

So far, you've learned that free will allows you to choose the condition of your garden and define your reality. Now you can choose to balance and blend these behaviors as well as expand your own leadership and your ability to work well with others. Understanding the survival and thriving tendencies, and the challenges of each leader behavior, gives you the power to be the natural cultivator of your garden. This will move you one step closer to your unique leadership expression with purpose and aim.

Exercise 3-A:
Spirit Blocker Identification Grid

On the next page, you will identify the truths you hold about yourself that block or empower your leadership spirit. Some of these truths may be what others have said about you that you have adopted as true. Complete the grid on the next page following these instructions:

1. In the "Truths" column, list everything you think about yourself that is true (i.e. I'm shy, attractive, unlovable, outgoing, difficult, bold, courageous, vivacious, etc.).
2. In the "Age" column write down how old you were when you first realized your truths. Think about the source event that instigated that feeling.
3. In the "Feeling/Emotion" column, describe the feeling you have about your truths. Place an S for seed or W for weed next to each feeling.
4. Subtract the age in the middle column from your current age and place that number in the "How Long" column. This is the number of years you have believed this truth about yourself. You may find it hard to give up some of your spirit blockers, depending upon how long you have held onto them. But remember, if it doesn't empower you, it may be time to weed it from your garden.
5. Draw a line through the truths that block your leadership spirit, and place a star or highlight those that empower you to be the best that you can be.

Sample:

TRUTH	AGE	FEELING/EMOTION	HOW LONG
I'm bold	16	Powerful—S	37 years
I'm not good enough	5	Scared—W	48 years

Spirit Blocker Identification Grid for _____

(Fill-in your name and current age)

TRUTH	AGE	FEELING/EMOTION	HOW LONG

Come back to this exercise and add to the list anytime you notice yourself thinking or saying a new "I am" statement.

If you have not completed the Leader Balance Inventory and Balance Wheel, do so now, otherwise go to Exercise 3-C.

EXERCISE 3-B*: LEADER BALANCE INVENTORY

Date: _____

Step One—Read across each row. Use each number from the rating scale *only* once in each row. See sample below:

Row 1	_4_ Problem solver	_1_ Sensible & logical	_2_ Good Listener	_3_ Negotiator

Rating Scale: *4 = most like you; 3 = somewhat like you; 2 = somewhat least like you; 1 = least like you.*

	COLUMN 1	COLUMN 2	COLUMN 3	COLUMN 4
Row 1	___ Problem solver	___ Sensible & logical	___ Good Listener	___ Negotiator
Row 2	___ Creative	___ Structured	___ Adaptable	___ Spontaneous
Row 3	___ Competent	___ Loyal	___ Appreciative	___ Playful
Row 4	___ Set the rules	___ Enforce the rules	___ Obey the rules	___ Avoid the rules
Row 5	___ Pacesetter	___ Decision maker	___ Supporter	___ Competitor
Row 6	___ Ideas	___ Process	___ Feelings	___ Action
Row 7	___ Dreamer	___ Practical	___ Understanding	___ Casual
Row 8	___ Asks "Why"	___ Asks "How"	___ Asks "Who"	___ Asks "What"
Row 9	___ Change	___ Results	___ Values	___ Freedom
Row 10	___ Build upon	___ Count on	___ Depend upon	___ Bet on
Row 11	___ Says "I think"	___ Says "I should"	___ Says "I feel"	___ Says "I know"
Row 12	___ Initiative	___ Direction	___ Guidance	___ Adventure
	_____ Total	_____ Total	_____ Total	_____ Total

29

Step Two—Add up the total in each column.

Step Three—Take the total score from each column and enter it on the line next to the corresponding column number on the Leader Balance Wheel. For example, the Column 1 score you enter on the Visualize Column 1 Score line. Then color in your score on each quadrant of the Balance Wheel to get a visual picture of your current leader balance.

*Leader Balance Exercise B Disclaimer: This exercise is not a psychological profile, nor scientifically validated and is only an indicator of how you responded to the Inventory at this particular time.

LEADER BALANCE WHEEL

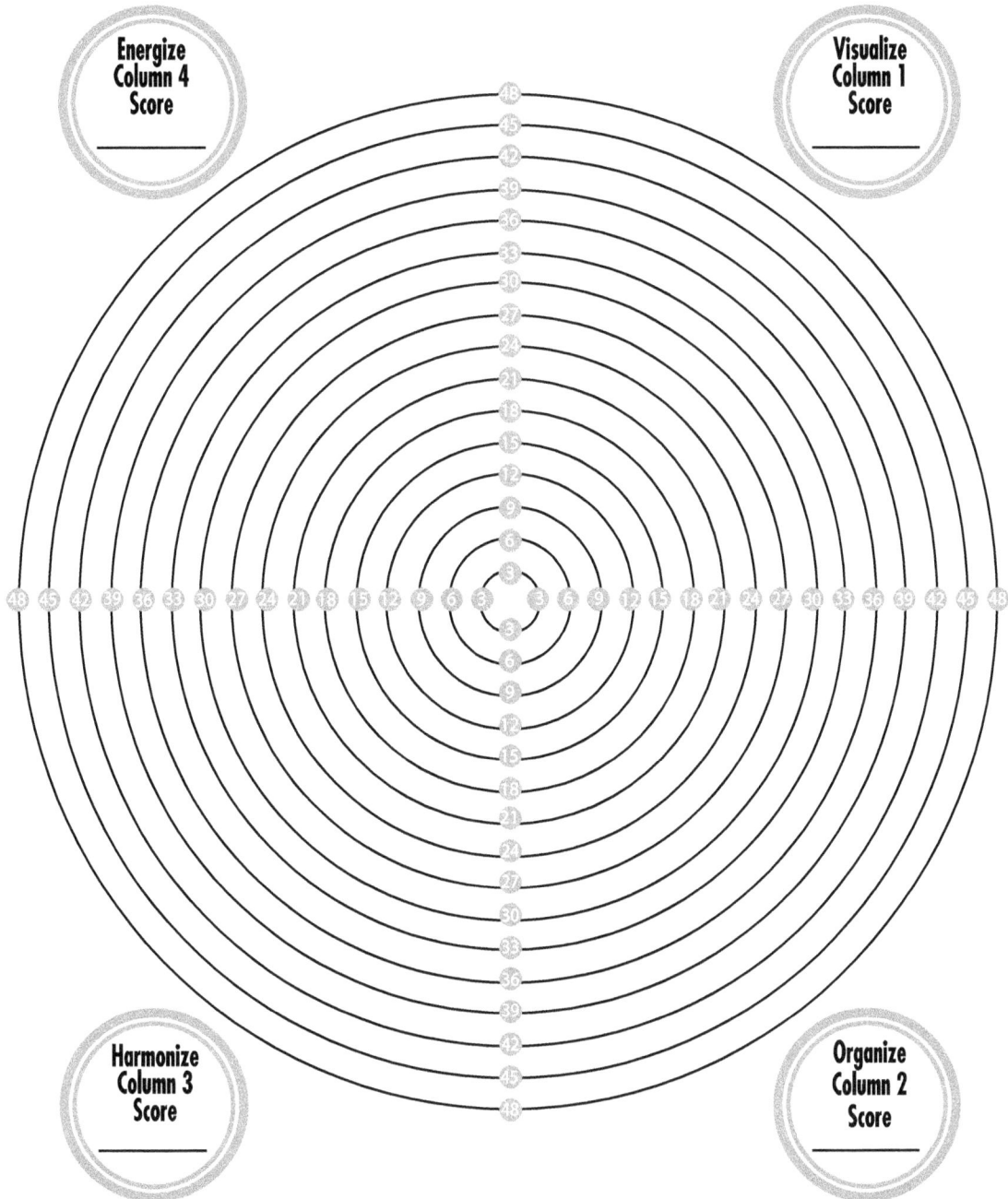

**Energize
Column 4
Score**
_____

**Visualize
Column 1
Score**
_____

**Harmonize
Column 3
Score**
_____

**Organize
Column 2
Score**
_____

48 45 42 39 36 33 30 27 24 21 18 15 12 9 6 3 3 6 9 12 15 18 21 24 27 30 33 36 39 42 45 48

48
45
42
39
36
33
30
27
24
21
18
15
12
9
6
3

3
6
9
12
15
18
21
24
27
30
33
36
39
42
45
48

EXERCISE 3-C:
THRIVING AND SURVIVING TENDENCIES

Fill in your name: _____

Circle the thriving and survival tendencies from the four leader behaviors you experience most often. Use this list to reinforce your thriving behaviors and as a reminder of when it's time to cultivate and weed your garden.

Thriving Tendencies

Visualize is **abstract** in nature and grows:
- thoughts
- inspiration
- imagination
- ideas
- vision for purpose and aim
- other _____

Organize is **concrete** in nature and grows:
- methodology
- order
- structure to fulfill goals
- other _____

Harmonize is **symbolic** in nature and grows:
- attunement
- coordination
- unity
- peace with inner self and others
- other _____

Energize is **literal** in nature and grows:
- play
- vitality
- strength
- joy for the adventure of life
- other _____

Surviving Tendencies

Visualize grows:
- dissatisfaction
- self-centeredness
- skepticism
- difficulty
- irritation
- frustration
- feelings of being overwhelmed

Organize grows:
- demands
- criticism
- self-righteousness
- insensitivity
- negativity
- control

Harmonize grows:
- impracticality
- defensiveness
- drama
- sensitivity
- disagreeableness
- distrust
- withdrawal

Energize grows:
- reactivity
- impatience
- inconsideration
- frustration
- disruptiveness
- anger
- cynicism
- impulsiveness

True leaders nurture yours and other's Leadership
Gardens to sprout greatness.
—Debra J. Slover

LESSON 4
NURTURING MEADOW

So far the lessons have focused primarily on Leadership Garden principles. Now the focus turns to the practices that are necessary to grow a thriving Leadership Garden. The following six leader-friendly gardening practices open your heart, bind you with others, and lift your spirits:

- Be nonjudgmental
- Do not enable
- Use empathy
- Prune gossip
- Eliminate blame
- Eradicate victimization

I'll begin with the first three practices. Forcing your opinions or personal values on others is toxic to your garden. *Being judgmental* separates you from others and robs you of love and appreciation. Suspend judgment, by separating the behavior from the person. This allows thoughts and communication about acceptable and unacceptable behaviors, without being self-righteous or *enabling* undesirable behavior. This requires skill in speaking and listening to others and that skill begins with empathy—the ability to listen to another's thoughts, feelings, and opinions without imposing your own on them.

You need to be responsible for your own thoughts and feelings, suspend judgment, and give up "being right" for the moment. In the heat of an argument this may be difficult, especially when you have strong beliefs, or a message you feel is important to convey. Suspending judgment of another, not always "being right," and really listening, works wonders.

Empathy is a bridge from survival to thriving leadership. It is a powerful way to interact with others. This subtle shift in thinking is strong fertilizer for Leadership Gardens. The more open and receptive you are to others, the more open and receptive they are to you. Remember, emotions and moods are contagious, and are at the root of most social friction or harmony.

Judgmental and *enabling* behaviors have the potential to destroy many personal, family, and professional relationships, and they thwart organizational, religious, environmental, and governmental missions. If you think about it, most wars and battles fought throughout history have been over personal, moral, religious, or political points of view. Imagine a world where empathy is the norm and leadership thrives. The good news—it can start with you.

The fourth leader-friendly gardening practice is to *prune gossip*. Expressing a negative opinion about someone in his or her absence is unkind. On the surface, it seems like a harmless form of entertainment, due to a lack of anything better to talk about. Unfortunately, talking about the faults or misfortunes of others makes some people feel better about their own life. A malicious character attack is similar to the destruction of your own and another's garden. However, the underbelly of gossip is that it diminishes your personal power and trust with others. A thriving leader does not engage in or tolerate gossip and prunes it when it begins.

The fifth practice is to *eliminate blame*—holding others responsible or at fault for something that you chose to participate in. Blame is a more severe form of gossip and a way to deflect personal responsibility. Taking 100% responsibility for your life eliminates blame and gives you personal power.

The sixth and most serious infection in a Leadership Garden is *victimization*. Blame and victimization often go hand-in-hand and can be devastating to a leader. Victimization is an unfortunate cultural phenomenon that is pervasive in today's society and takes the attention away from those who are the true victims. Victims need support to heal and restore their power, not to be rendered helpless and diminished, leaving them even more victimized. Victimization is a form of survival leadership that robs you of the opportunity to be in control of, and responsible for, how you *experience* life. The following are victim-like behaviors that infect Leadership Gardens:

- Blaming others
- Being morally right and making others wrong
- Shirking responsibility
- Feeling entitled to sympathy because of your misfortunes
- Righteous indignation for being wronged

Using these six leaders-friendly gardening practices may well be the most difficult aspect of growing a Leadership Garden. Yet these practices have the greatest potential for uplifting the human spirit and creating a thriving world where love and empathy reign.

The challenge in using the leader-friendly gardening practices comes from the inability to separate the person from the behavior, and discern *real* from *imagined* life-threatening danger. When your survival instinct kicks in, you automatically respond in one of three ways: *fight, flee, or freeze*. Remember, behaviors are learned and practiced over time and are adapted by you so can survive the world around you. The more you practice survival behaviors that are ego motivated the more they become your way of life.

The irony of being human is you are born, you live, and you die, therefore you will not survive life. What separates you from other animal life is the ability to choose your behavior and the Leadership Garden condition is which you live.

Up to this point, I have mostly addressed the personal impact of leader-friendly gardening practices. On a larger scale, gossip, blame, and fear mongering for monetary gain is standard tabloid, mass entertainment, and is today's news. This does little to elevate the spirit of humans, to feel positive and do much needed good in the world. Yet it is part of the landscape in which we live.

Your Leadership Garden will not thrive alone or in isolation. There are too many social and environmental factors out of your control. However, you can do your part to create a new conversation that creates fertile ground for leaders to flourish, and back it by becoming a member of the Leadership Garden Registry.

The Registry is the place where individuals, non-profit entities, and businesses meet to seed and nurture Leadership Gardens and support leader-friendly gardening practices.

Leader-friendly gardening practices help you carry out thriving behaviors. These thriving behaviors will require a conscious and consistent effort to override the automatic survival behavior of all human beings.

To assist you, as part of the Leadership Garden Legacy family, we have also established the Leadership Garden Fund. The Fund will provide Cultivation Grants to create "Practice Projects" in the following categories:

- Inclusion Projects—*Be nonjudgmental*
- Safe and Healthy Community Projects—*Do not enable*
- Compassion Projects—*Use empathy*
- Kindness Projects—*Prune gossip*
- Accountability Projects—*Eliminate blame*
- Healing Projects—*Eradicate victimization*

In the meantime, Exercise 4 will help you evaluate the condition of your Leadership Garden, and help you choose the leader-friendly gardening practices that you will apply to alter the relationships and situations in your life that are not thriving.

Keep in mind you cannot alter another's behavior. You can only choose to make your behavior grow and develop, and then connect with others who want to do the same. You can, however, always use empathy in any given circumstance as a bridge from survival to thriving leadership and move yourself forward.

EXERCISE 4: NURTURE TIME

A) Write down the name of someone *important* to you with whom you have had differences:

Person: _____

List what you see in their behavior you don't like: _____

_____

_____

_____

_____

Now list what you see in your own behavior that you don't like: _____

_____

_____

_____

_____

Circle any behaviors that are similar between the two of you.

Please note: Often what you do not like about others, you do not like about yourself. If this person is close to you, ask them to take the Leader Balance Inventory and complete their Balance Wheel to see how you are similar or where your survival leader behavior tendencies may have clashed.

Let go of your defenses and be honest with yourself. See where judgment, gossip, blame, or victimization may be infecting your relationship with this person. List the leader-friendly gardening practices you will use to alter your view of the relationship: _____

_____

_____

_____

B) Now identify a situation that is *important* to you that you don't like and answer as in the person exercise:

Situation: _____

Identify behaviors used by other in the situation that you don't like: _____

_____

_____

_____

_____

_____

List what behaviors you are using that are similar:_____

_____

_____

_____

_____

_____

List the leader-friendly gardening practices you will now use to alter your view of the situation: _____

_____

_____

_____

_____

_____

Please note: To increase your proficiency recognizing the condition of your Leadership Garden, return to this exercise whenever you face conflict, or are in an uncomfortable situation. Combine this with the Reality Check exercise from Lesson 2 on page 15.

Leaders blossom and thrive with a personal purpose and aim.
–Debra J. Slover

LESSON 5
INVENTIVE ROOST

In the first lesson, you learned that your spirit lives in the values, conscience, attitudes, and principles that promote thoughts, actions, and purpose. The next task in the Leadership Garden is to formulate your purpose and aim. This will become a phenomenon of your own unique self-expression, and allow your leader spirit to grow and blossom. When you discover and express your purpose, leadership takes on new meaning.

Inventing a unique purpose and aim that inspires, guides, and directs you through life, requires that you devise new ways of *being* the leader of your life.

If you are stuck in a pattern of trying to succeed, in order to obtain happiness, satisfaction, or personal fulfillment *some day*, you will miss the opportunity to experience the joy of *being* a leader today. You will have become a person who defines who you A.R.E. by what you DO. This makes you a *human doing*, rather than a *human being*.

Are E.A.R.S. necessary? Absolutely!

- **A** stands for action
- **R** stands for result
- **E** stands for experience

Your way of *being* is truly all you have to help you produce the results you desire with grace and ease. Leadership, with a unique purpose and aim is an honor and a privilege. This privilege belongs to the *human being* who makes a difference in the world every day.

In a survival condition, the joy, satisfaction, and fulfillment of *being* a leader is masked by the tremendous effort it takes to protect your ego, and maintain control over your domain. When leadership is viewed this way, it's no wonder so many step back and let someone else lead. But it doesn't have to be that way.

In a thriving Leadership Garden, work becomes an extension of the experience you create. To invent your unique purpose and aim and develop new ways of being, you simply scramble A.R.E. and add an S at the end:

- **E** stands for experience
- **A** stands for action
- **R** stands for result
- **S** stands for synergy

When you start with the *experience* you want, and take *actions* consistent with that experience, the *results* you achieve will improve exponentially. It's the synergy of all three—starting with a new way of *being* that will give you the ability to listen for, speak to, and act upon what inspires you—while enjoying the process of leading your life as a *human being*.

EXERCISE 5:
INVENTING YOUR PURPOSE AND AIM

Step 1: In the chart below list the *experiences* (feelings/emotions) that inspire you and those that dispirit you. If you run out of room in the space provided on each grid use the space provided on each side.

Experiences

INSPIRING	DISPIRITING

Now circle the one or two words that most inspire you.

Step 2: List the *actions* you take daily, weekly, or monthly. List what you enjoy and what you avoid.

Actions

ENJOY	AVOID

Now circle the one or two actions that you most enjoy.

Step 3: List the *results* you desire and need in your life. You can go back to page 7 to cross-reference your wants and your desires here. Be sure to distinguish clearly for yourself those things you desire versus what you actually need to live. You will probably notice your actual needs are rather small compared to your desires. This is normal human behavior so don't despair.

Results

DESIRES	NEEDS

Now circle the one or two results you most desire.

Step 4: Play with the words you circled from each chart and write your purpose statement, then continue with step five.

My purpose in life is _____

_____

_____

_____

Please note: If you are having trouble coming up with a purpose statement that inspires you, there may be some hidden weeds or spirit blockers left in your Leadership Garden, or survival leader behaviors to cultivate. Don't let what dispirits you or what you avoid cloud your imagination or get caught in the acquisition trap of material things you desire. Think in terms of an experience you have had where you took an action that made a difference you desired and it had nothing to do with obtaining a material thing.

You may need to reflect for a while and let this exercise simmer. If so, remember purpose hatches new behaviors. Once you have your purpose statement, you will know and feel it.

Step 5: Finally, add *synergy* to determine your aim. List how, with whom, and where you want to express your purpose. Circle your targets (how, who, and where) and combine them with your purpose statement to create your aim.

Aim

HOW	WHO	WHERE

Step 6: Now create your purpose and aim statement to include who, how, and where.

My purpose and aim is _____

_____

_____

_____

Your aim may shift over time as your purpose becomes more clear. If you struggle with discontent inside, check back here to see if you have slipped back into a survival *human doing* mode.

Allow the famous quote below to be a daily reminder as you begin to live your unique purpose and aim.

You are never given a wish or dream without also
being given the power to make it come true.
—Richard Bach

43

NOTES

_____
_____
_____
_____
_____
_____
_____
_____
_____
_____
_____
_____
_____
_____
_____
_____
_____
_____
_____
_____
_____
_____
_____
_____
_____
_____
_____
_____
_____

Integrity brings out the quality and greatness in leaders.
—Debra J. Slover

LESSON 6
QUALITY YARD

Integrity, the next principle of the Leadership Garden, determines the quality of a leader. Leadership Gardens thrive with integrity, and wither and die without it. Regardless of your thoughts and feelings in the moment, you bring integrity to who you are as a *human being* when your words and actions are consistent with your purpose and aim.

Integrity is the "golden egg" of leadership. The golden egg is a symbol of your word, a leader's most prized possession.

If your garden is in a survival condition, you make up excuses, cut corners, or sell out, and may revert to harsh judgments, blame, or victimization. It is important to remember that you have the innate ability to make up anything to suit your needs. What you make up will either reinforce a survival condition or empower you to thrive. It is always your choice.

When you bring integrity into your life, growing a thriving Leadership Garden is organic and gives you a sense of rightness. This is distinct from self-righteousness which is toxic to your Leadership Garden.

When the golden of egg of integrity is missing, you feel a nagging discontent that alerts you to rebalance your four leader behaviors and/or use leader-friendly gardening practices in order to regain your sense of rightness.

Along with integrity, there are seven common attributes of leadership. Each attribute has several aspects and is an insight into the way you tend to express your leader behavior. But who you really are surfaces when you balance and blend the attributes to express your genuine purpose and aim with others. The attributes are defined as follows:

- **Communication:** Exchange of thoughts, ideas, information, and/or feelings
- **Cooperation:** Working with another for mutual benefit
- **Recognition:** State of being seen, known, or heard
- **Respect:** Acceptance, courtesy, or honor
- **Responsibility:** Accountability for thoughts, feelings, actions, or results
- **Teamwork:** The combined interest and talent of a group working to achieve a common goal
- **Trust:** Reliance, integrity, certainty, or confidence

Keep in mind, the goals you set and the actions you take will not thrive without integrity, the guiding force that builds strength in you and trust with others. Integrity allows you to grow, expand, and develop the essential attributes needed to blossom your leadership greatness.

EXERCISE 6: PICK YOUR ATTRIBUTES

Step 1: To provide the first set of skills and practices for your purpose and aim, go back to your Leader Balance Inventory on page 29. On the chart below now *circle* the word/statements you originally picked on page 29 that you said were most like you (with the number 4).

For example, in **"row one"** the attribute is **"Cooperation."** You may have picked **"Problem solver"** a visualize behavior that is most like you. To help with this identification process, the row number is in the right column on the chart below and on the left column of your original inventory.

ATTRIBUTES	VISUALIZE	ORGANIZE	HARMONIZE	ENERGIZE	ROW
Communication	Asks "Why"	Asks "How"	Asks "Who"	Asks "What"	8
Communication	Says "I think"	Says "I should"	Says "I feel"	Says "I know"	11
Cooperation	Sets rules	Enforces rules	Obeys rules	Avoids rules	4
Cooperation	Problem solver	Sensible & logical	Good listener	Negotiator	1
Recognition	Competent	Loyal	Appreciative	Playful	3
Respect	Change	Results	Values	Freedom	9
Respect	Creative	Structured	Adaptable	Spontaneous	2
Responsibility	Pacesetter	Decision maker	Supporter	Competitor	5
Responsibility	Initiative	Direction	Guidance	Adventure	12
Teamwork	Ideas	Process	Feelings	Action	6
Teamwork	Dreamer	Practical	Understanding	Casual	7
Trust	Build upon	Count on	Depend upon	Bet on	10
Total Score					
Most Like You					

a) Transfer your total score from your inventory (page 29) in the row "Total Score."

b) Add the total score of the **Visualize** and **Organize** column_____. Add the total score of the **Harmonize** and **Energize** columns_____.

c) Now multiply by 4 the number of word/phrases you circled in each column. Enter that in the row "Most like you." Move on to Step 2.

Step 2: Write your Purpose and Aim Statement below: _____

_____

_____

On this Inventory, you will now choose the behaviors that will be **most useful** to empower your purpose and aim statement. If they support your statement, they may be the same behaviors as your previous choices. But remember, leader behaviors are not fixed, and you can choose new behaviors at any time. Use the rating scale below to rescore your inventory:

Useful Rating Scale: *4 = most useful; 3 = somewhat useful; 2 = somewhat not useful. 1 = least useful.*

To use Asli's example in the fable of the book, when she learned to say "I feel" instead of "I know" she chose to practice new "communication harmonize behavior" that matched her purpose and aim.

ATTRIBUTES	VISUALIZE	ORGANIZE	HARMONIZE	ENERGIZE	ROW
Communication	__Asks "Why"	__Asks "How"	__Asks "Who"	__Asks "What"	8
Communication	__Says "I think"	__Says "I should"	__Says "I feel"	__Says "I know"	11
Cooperation	__Sets rules	__Enforces rules	__Obeys rules	__Avoids rules	4
Cooperation	__Problem solver	__Sensible & logical	__Good listener	__Negotiator	1
Recognition	__Competent	__Loyal	__Appreciative	__Playful	3
Respect	__Change	__Results	__Values	__Freedom	9
Respect	__Creative	__Structured	__Adaptable	__Spontaneous	2
Responsibility	__Pacesetter	__Decision maker	__Supporter	__Competitor	5
Responsibility	__Initiative	__Direction	__Guidance	__Adventure	12
Teamwork	__Ideas	__Process	__Feelings	__Action	6
Teamwork	__Dreamer	__Practical	__Understanding	__Casual	7
Trust	__Build upon	__Count on	__Depend upon	__Bet on	10
New Total					
*Most Useful					

Step 3:

    a: Add up your new scores and write them in the "New Total" columns for each leader behavior column.

    b) Add the new total score of the **Visualize** and **Organize** column_____. Add the new total score of the **Harmonize** and **Energize** columns_____.

    c) Now circle all those you scored **4=most useful** in each column. Multiply the number you circled in each column by 4 and enter that number in the *Most Useful Row.

Step 4: Transfer your "New Total" scores from the previous page, to the Purpose and Aim Leader Balance Wheel—New Attributes on the next page. Complete your Purpose and Aim—Leader Balance Wheel. Then return to Step 5.

Step 5: Remember—*visualize* and *organize* are direction-oriented behaviors, and *harmonize* and *energize* are guidance-oriented behaviors. The first inventory was designed to help identify the behaviors and the orientation you use most often *without* a purpose and aim in mind. You now have a visual picture of the attributes you chose that will empower your unique purpose and aim.

Beware of those who subscribe to the notion that behaviors are genetically fixed. Even if that were the case, we now know about the brain's ability to rewire itself. The rewiring process takes place through conscious thought and the practice of new behaviors you desire.

Summarize below what you discovered about picking new leader behaviors that support your purpose and aim statement.

_____

_____

_____

_____

_____

_____

_____

_____

_____

PURPOSE AND AIM
LEADER BALANCE WHEEL—NEW ATTRIBUTES

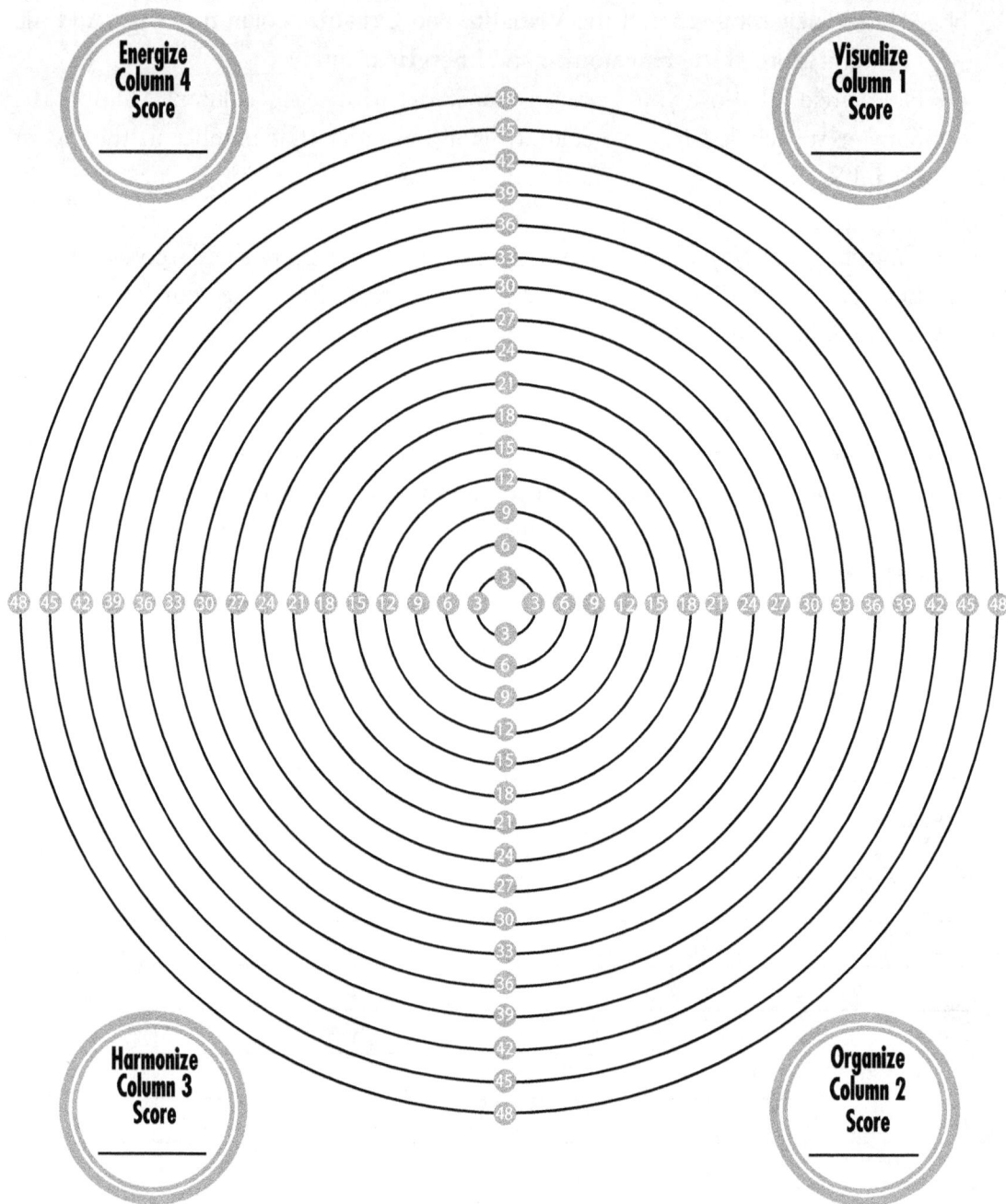

**Energize
Column 4
Score**

_____

**Visualize
Column 1
Score**

_____

48
45
42
39
36
33
30
27
24
21
18
15
12
9
6
3

48 45 42 39 36 33 30 27 24 21 18 15 12 9 6 3   3 6 9 12 15 18 21 24 27 30 33 36 39 42 45 48

3
6
9
12
15
18
21
24
27
30
33
36
39
42
45
48

**Harmonize
Column 3
Score**

_____

**Organize
Column 2
Score**

_____

50

Leaders who commit to a genuine purpose and aim
will thrive under any storm life has to offer.
—Debra J. Slover

LESSON 7
UNSTOPPABLE PASTURE

Commitment is the next principle in the Leadership Garden. In this lesson you look at physical, social, emotional, and spiritual boundaries that are designed to provide protection, safety, and order to life, and are necessary for basic survival. Some of these boundaries are:

- Physical needs such as food, clothing, shelter, and health
- Social laws and norms that govern society
- Emotional connections and interactions with others
- Spiritual beliefs and values that guide your conscience

To thrive, it is important to understand and respect these boundaries. The focus in this lesson is on self-imposed emotional boundaries that can turn into barriers of self-doubt, fear of failure, resignation, or cynicism. These are the barriers that suppress your leadership voice, dampen your spirit, and stunt your growth.

It's useful to look at opposing views, but when you're in a thriving condition you don't let the views of others sway you from your unique purpose and aim. Because unexpected setbacks and obstacles often occur, and failure is a part of life, you may find yourself in a resigned and cynical survival condition. Setbacks, failure, and disappointments are to be expected, and thriving leaders use them as an opportunity to grow and expand.

Unstoppable commitment, with integrity toward your unique purpose and aim, counterbalances your barriers and will inspire and free your leadership spirit. However, being unstoppable does not give you a license to be stubborn or foolish. It is one thing to *say* you are committed to something, and yet another to *be* committed enough to stand up for it, and take the action you need to make it a reality.

The key to being unstoppable is to let go of your ego and move through the four essential steps in the "Circle of Commitment": *declare, act, complete,* and *celebrate.* Using all four leader behaviors helps you move through the circle with ease. However, when you are under stress or up against deadlines, it's easy to revert back to familiar behavior, and you may get stuck. Below are the leader behaviors and the phases for each that could cause problems:

- **Visualize**—*declaration* phase. New ideas and projects are easy, but committing the time and resources to complete them, and then celebrate, is a challenge.
- **Energize**—*action* phase. There is a tendency to abandon the project if it isn't fun or doesn't have enough action.
- **Organize**—*completion* phase. The desire to produce results overrides the need to celebrate and experience the joy of the journey.
- **Harmonize**—*celebration* phase. There is a tendency to revel in the joy and to resist getting back to business.

In addition to these problems, there is another hidden barrier to commitment, what I call the, "Commitment Paradox." Most leadership comes with a sense of obligation and attachment, but a thriving leader commits to a purpose and aim without either. The Commitment Paradox relates to your integrity. In a survival condition, your integrity is compromised by an *obligation* that turns into martyrdom and/or an *attachment* to an outcome that limits your ability to be flexible and adaptable. That's when you may find you're stopped.

When you give up unwholesome attachments and obligations, live your life with integrity, and are true to your purpose and aim, unforeseen opportunities will emerge and new results will occur. Since every leader faces obstacles, setbacks, and disagreement from others, the question is, will you give up, survive, or thrive? Even when you face what seems like insurmountable odds, your leadership will thrive when you remove your self-imposed barriers and remain steadfast, flexible, and open to your unique purpose and aim.

COMMITMENT PARADOX

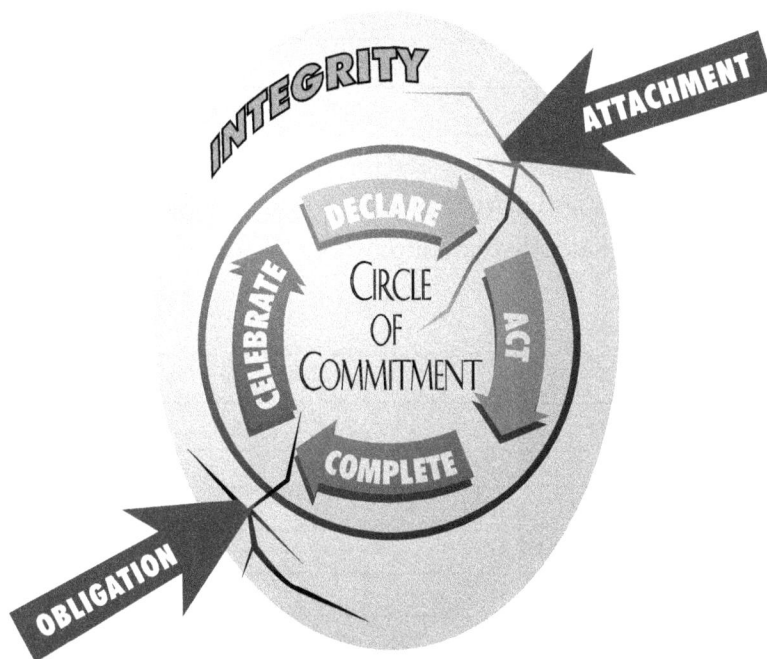

INTEGRITY

ATTACHMENT

DECLARE

CELEBRATE

CIRCLE OF COMMITMENT

ACT

COMPLETE

OBLIGATION

EXERCISE 7: BREAK FREE

Step 1: List the emotional barriers that may stop you from committing to your purpose and aim. List any unwholesome attachment or obligations you may have to an outcome.

EMOTIONAL BARRIERS	ATTACHMENT	OBLIGATION

Step 2: Identify where you may be caught in the Circle of Commitment, based upon your survival leader behavior tendencies: _____

_____

_____

_____

Step 3: Now, take the action necessary to commit to your purpose and aim. Create at least one goal and then a list of actions (what, how, who, and where) with suitable deadlines.

Goal: _____

_____

_____

ACTIONS	BY WHEN

Goal: _____
_____
_____

ACTIONS	BY WHEN

Goal: _____
_____
_____

ACTIONS	BY WHEN

Goal: _____
_____
_____

ACTIONS	BY WHEN

NOTES

*A thriving leader spirit sings
so others can hear the song of greatness.*
–Debra J. Slover

LESSON 8
EXPRESSION PEN

The Introduction began with the Leadership Garden Legacy quote about sprouting greatness. Greatness sprouts from the communication of your self-expression, the last principle of the Leadership Garden. Your unique self-expression blossoms when your purpose and aim bind your heart, mind, and spirit into a new "way of being" that communicates greatness.

Defined in Lesson 6, communication is the exchange of thoughts, ideas, information, or feelings that occur through your words, listening ability, and behavior. Communication is the instrument of your integrity and the other attributes of leadership.

In a survival condition, your integrity is compromised by how you listen, speak, and react to your thoughts. Those reactions and thoughts are controlled by your past experiences, as discussed in Chapter 2. The past is a vantage point from which you can only compare, assess, and judge what you hear and see. When in a survival mode what is actually said and happening around you is lost. You miss the opportunity to see, hear, learn, and imagine anything new. In other words, *past* experiences do inform you and help you learn from your mistakes. But they are not the most useful guide, due to the limits they place upon your ability to create your *future*.

The weeds that we have discussed in the previous chapters block your ability to listen. You remove these weeds when you learn to communicate new thoughts, feelings, and actions that demonstrate your greatness and open the door for the greatness of others. Transforming *how* you listen and *what* you listen for, creates a new opportunity for your words and actions.

When you hear, see, think about, and respond to excitement or stress with words and actions, your dominant verbal communication tendencies may take over. Below is a list of those tendencies for each leader behavior:

- **Visualize** says, "I think," and asks, "Why?"
- **Organize** says, "I should," and asks, "How?"
- **Harmonize** says, "I feel," and asks, "Who?"
- **Energize** says, "I know," and asks, "What?"

Practicing your purpose and aim with integrity creates a condition for greatness; you facilitate (or support) better communication and behaviors that nurture your greatness and that of others.

When you paint a picture in your mind of what is possible to achieve with your purpose and aim—the essence of who you are—you listen for, speak to, and respond to only that. If your communication touches the mind, heart, and spirit of others, they naturally join in. If your communication fails to have the desired impact, you also take responsibility for that. Who you are and what you listen for, combined with how you listen, think, speak, and behave, creates the synergy for greatness. One idea leads to another, which leads to action, and actions that grow in harmony with others sprout your greatness.

Growing and nurturing a thriving Leadership Garden enables you to clear your mind and re-write your legacy, giving you the ability to hear and speak your unique voice. When you choose to become a thriving leader with a unique purpose and aim, and practice the principles and exercises in this guidebook, your garden, and the gardens of those around you, will flourish.

Congratulations. You have now completed a vital step toward the blossoming of your unique *Leadership Garden Legacy.* The direction you take, and what you see and listen for, will guide your behavior. The power you have to choose your legacy and write your life story is the favor, grace, and beauty of your life. To support you on your new journey, complete the final exercise on the next page.

EXERCISE 8: TIME TO COMMUNICATE

Step 1: Go back to page 7 in your guidebook and review your "What I Want in My Life" list. Now that you have your purpose and aim, it's time to take action. Make a list of opportunities that you now see. Begin with what you truly want in life. What will you do and with whom will you communicate your purpose and aim?

OPPORTUNITY	ACTION	WITH WHOM

Step 2: Next, make a list of any unfinished business you would like to complete and with whom you would like to communicate.

UNFINISHED BUSINESS	I'LL COMMUNICATE WITH	BY WHEN

Step 3: You will not thrive alone or in isolation. Make a list of people with whom you will share your purpose and aim. Then, ask for their support. Doing this will help you achieve your goals and actions.

Every good idea or intention must be backed up by a specific action that can be measured in time and space. Communication with and support from the people you love, trust, and respect the most will help your leadership blossom.

PEOPLE	SUPPORT	BY WHEN

You have now reached the communication gateway that will sprout your leadership greatness. Honor your word to yourself, communicate with those on your list, and ask for their support.

By taking the responsibility to guide and direct your life and the actions you have outlined in this guidebook, I promise you'll be amazed at the unforeseen opportunities that come your way, and the results that you will sprout.

I end this guidebook with **What's Next—Empower Your Future** and a short story to illustrate this point. Before I do, I wish to close this section with a passage from the Epilogue of my book:

> My friend, Edwardo, mentioned in Chapter Seven [of my book], died at the young age of 41, before I finished. . . We often said that leadership is not about us, but about making a difference for others. Yet leadership is all about how we lead our life, for how can we make a difference for others if we don't know how important we are, and understand the profound impact we have on those around us?
>
> As you embark on your new journey of unique leadership expression, I leave you with Edwardo's last words to me, *"Keep the drafts coming. I truly enjoy witnessing the creative process. It's like witnessing God, for me. I love you."*

NOTES

WHAT'S NEXT?
EMPOWER YOUR FUTURE

Our goal is to seed and nurture 11 million Leadership Gardens by 11/11/11. Why such an audacious goal?

I have an undying commitment to make the world a thriving place to live, work, and play in—now and for future generations.

I believe there is not a person or problem on this planet that would not be positively impacted by the use of *at least* one of the six leader-friendly gardening practices. I base this upon more than 30 years of professional and personal experience training and empowering youth and adult leaders. In keeping with this belief, I have established the Leadership Garden Fund. This fund will supply Cultivation Grants to support leader-friendly gardening "Practice Projects:"

- Inclusion Projects—Be nonjudgmental
- Safe and Healthy Community Projects—Do not enable
- Compassion Projects—Use empathy
- Kindness projects—Prune gossip
- Accountability projects—Eliminate blame
- Healing Projects—Eradicate Victimization

Imagine a world where these practices are the norm, versus weed-like survival behaviors that lead to judgmental behavior, gossip, blame, and victimization.

The fund is intended to support an online registry of individuals, organizations, and businesses that desire to make a difference as a global family.

By becoming a Leadership Garden Registry member, you help reverse the downward spiral of human behavior and environmental destruction, to an upward motion of the greatest human potential, beginning with yourself and the people around you.

To help you understand why I believe so strongly in standing steadfast to your commitment to a unique purpose and aim, I'll share the story that set in motion the creation of the Leadership Garden Legacy online community Registry, the offline Practice Grants, and this guidebook.

While I have written a book, held a vision, and created a community/philanthropic/business structure, the inspiration for my goal began with love and commitment to the grown son of just one mother/grandmother named Jeanne. Her story follows.

Providence at Play

On January 20, 2007, a beautiful winter day in Oregon, Jeanne Beattie, a retired elementary school teacher from Eastern Washington was visiting the Oregon Coast with her husband and friends. They went for lunch at the renowned Canyon Way Restaurant and Bookstore in Newport. While waiting in line to be seated, Jeannie spotted *U.N.I.Q.U.E.: Growing the Leader Within,* sitting on the counter next to the cash register. I was there with my new book doing a book signing. With her son in mind, she read the first paragraph of the back cover and purchased the book for him. She told me her son, Mark, was a doctoral candidate in Leadership Studies at Gonzaga University, in Spokane, Washington, and as we chatted, she told me of his global vision. He loved to garden and she thought he would enjoy my Leadership Garden metaphor.

Mark read the book and just as his mother suspected, it combined his passion for gardening and servant leadership. That summer, he created and conducted a Service-Learning course in the Bachelor of General Studies (BGS) Program at Gonzaga University. The learning objectives of the course began with personal journaling using the exercises outlined in my book as the required text.

During the Leadership Garden Course, the students planted an actual garden, and the produce was donated to the Spokane Valley Food Bank. The students also learned global issues around food, including water scarcity, genetic modification, food safety, and sustainable economics. It was Mark's goal to have his students *think globally* and *act locally.*

Students involved in the course were nontraditional students over 25, most with families and working full-time while attaining degrees. One student remarked in the *Spokane Review*'s newspaper story about the course, "The text has been great. It gives you the opportunity for self-reflection, to get rid of the weeds in your life . . . . It's neat to get out of the classroom, and do something."

I had the pleasure of visiting Mark and the students in the garden that summer. Inspired by Mark's effort, I shared my audacious goal with him and his students. I also presented the students with Inaugural Leadership Gardener certificates, plus a Leadership Garden metal sculpture to adorn their garden.

The book topic of the day was the Nurturing Meadow, emphasizing the six leader-friendly gardening practices. The garden topic was to create and learn how to build compost. Fresh manure from the horse pasture next door, grass clippings, and straw were used.

The connection between the composting lesson and the need to fertilize new leader behavior, using the six leader-friendly gardening practices, made me chuckle. *I likened harsh judgments, gossip, and blame to manure in the human Leadership Garden. It has odors that perpetuate victimization and we need to recycle such behaviors globally and fertilize something new.* That planted the seed for the Leadership Garden Registry. I left that day, renewed and inspired by Mark and his students.

In the fall, I followed Mark by email on his adventure to Africa. He planned to do his dissertation on *The Role of Education in Economic Development: A Phenomenological Study through NetTel@Africa*, at the University of Dar es Salaam in Tanzania.

Mark learned first hand: no electricity, no teachers, no books, no computers *equal* no education. When he visited the head matron of a nearby and recently built school, he asked about computers, she asked about electricity. The school had a 450-student waiting list to begin secondary school. The building was missing the necessary infrastructure: electricity, water, teachers, desks, and books. The village had just received its first water tank a few weeks before.

Mark became aware of the need to assist countries whose economic and political situations precluded the introduction of systems that would achieve their goal of education for all. He maintained that via the worldwide web, a network of individuals with similar interests could make a difference.

I learned from Mark how important—really crucial—gardens are to the people who live and work there. He described how a doctor at the hospital did surgery in the morning, and then went to work in the garden in the afternoon, so there would be food for the patients.

This tugged on my heart strings and deepened my passion. I saw an opportunity and felt a strong need to help seed and nurture Leadership Gardens in parts of the world that desperately lacked resources. The stories Mark was sharing reconfirmed my belief in the power of the human spirit to rise up in less than ideal circumstances. I donated copies of my book for him to share and to help reinforce the internal strength and power these people demonstrated.

On my next visit to Spokane that spring, I met with Mark. He proudly shared his African adventure and photos of the people he had grown to love as his global family. Some were now part of what he called my budding book club.

One young woman had a dream of becoming a librarian. He gave her the book to empower her dream and begin her library collection.

Another shared with Mark by email, "I finished reading the book you gave me. It is a nice book. I really liked it. It gave me a lot of courage. I'm now UNIQUE, walking boldly in the garden of leadership. Thanks again for the book."

His sharing warmed my heart and lifted my spirit. I requested permission from Mark to communicate with this gentleman personally. He wrote back:

Dear Debra Slover,

My name is Mramba Makange Manyelo, I am a trainer in finance. Mark told me briefly who you are. I can imagine the wonderful person I am linked to. Mark is also UNIQUE to know that I wished to hear direct from you. For sure your book is unique in the sense that the reader can just read it as a novel, but unlike the love and action novels the communicated message is very professional and academically designed. You wrote it in a manner that the reader keeps on reflecting to his or her own mistakes and gears himself or herself towards correction of the previous mistakes and prepares to walk ahead.

It is unfortunate that the book was borrowed by one of my friends; otherwise I would be grateful to give you some quotes from the book that I consider very educative.

I keep on encouraging you to extend your distribution to Tanzania and other African countries. This is a book that is very suitable for the young generation in colleges and universities because it is able to change the attitude of a person in a very short span of time. (You are allowed to quote me)

Let us keep in touch.

Kind regards,
Mramba

After seeing the pictures of the people Mark had touched and shared my book with, I began to look for ways to build the online infrastructure much like Mark said, ". . . via the worldwide web, a network of individuals with similar interests would make a difference."

But I also knew the internet cannot replace the face-to-face exchange of energy that allows two human beings to create a deeper meaning. I was connected more deeply to Mramba now, not because of our internet exchange, but because of the pride and energy Mark showed sharing his pictures. The smile on his face spoke volumes.

Now the next seed was planted. The Leadership Garden Registry was born to support a worldwide network of information and communication exchange with like-minded people around the globe that I had just met in those pictures.

The Leadership Garden Fund was created as my way to support this face-to-face human exchange. In addition, the guidebook is designed to empower individuals to lead this process right in their own home, community, or workplace, using the Leadership Garden empowerment tools.

The final tool is the fall release of the children's full color adaptation called *U.N.I.Q.U.E. KIDS: Growing My Leadership Garden.* This will aid grandparents, parents, teachers and others in the empowerment of children.

I declared that 2009 would be the time for Leadership Gardens to shine, not only online, but face-to-face in real time.

I have the utmost faith in your ability to share the wisdom that you have gained by your own life experiences. I turn my desire and power to seed and nurture your Leadership Garden back to you. Together we can reverse the downward spiral of human behavior and environmental destruction that prevails today and create a thriving future for generations to come.

This new vision sprouted from my chance meeting face-to-face with Jeanne, a mother, grandmother, and a teacher herself, and the friendship that ensued with her son.

The irony to the story:

The day I met Jeanne was my first official bookstore signing. Hers was the *only* book I sold that day. Before I headed to the coast, I had promised myself it would be a joyous day, regardless of the outcome. I was given the opportunity to plant some Leadership Garden seeds. And that I did—just one.

I thought back to how meeting Jeanne set in motion a chain of events that I had not planned and could not imagine. The point of my story is to illustrate that one moment in time, one human being, and one simple action can make a difference that alters the course of one person's entire life journey. When I asked Mark why he chose my book and created the course, he simply said, "providence at play."

The Leadership Garden Registry is the place where your efforts help to expand the reach of a positive human face-to-face exchange.

I invite you to join with me and help write the next chapter of the Leadership Garden Legacy, as you carve out your own unique legacy. Trust me, there's no telling what will happen.

If I have learned one thing about life it is this: regardless of all your well-intentioned plans and actions you take, some things are still best left in the hands of fate. All you can really do is *live* your unique leadership legacy.

Not all those who wander are lost.
—J.R.R. Tolkien

NOTES

The End

Your U.N.I.Q.U.E. Leadership Garden

The miracle of life
is to thrive on the journey
with purpose and aim;
the endnote is
your spirit lives on.
–Debra. J. Slover

LEADERSHIP GARDEN REGISTRY

Introductory Member Benefits:

Sign up for our free eBook online at *www.leadershipgardenlegacy.com*
No obligation and no fee

Lifetime Member Benefits:

- Free MP3 download of the Leadership Garden empowerment audio book *U.N.I.Q.U.E. Growing the Leader Within* (regularly 24.95)
- 11% discount on all products and services. Ask about quantity discounts for 50 or more items.
- Your own **profile page** to share your stories and network with other members
- Members only eligibility for Cultivation Grants from the Leadership Garden Fund (Must be a not-for-profit, school, or institution or have a *sponsor member group)

LIFETIME MEMBERSHIP	FEE	FUND SHARE
Individual/Family	$30	$10
Group or Organization	$60	$20
Business: under 50 employees:	$100	$40
over 50 employees	$200	$60

*An individual member can apply for a grant but must have a sponsorship non-profit group. For example, a grandparent wants to work with a grandchild's school to conduct a Practice Project idea the grandparent and grandchild created.

Patron Donor Member Benefits:

All benefits included in level one membership plus:

- A tax deductible donation letter directly from the Calvert Foundation. Patron fees are deposited directly into the irrevocable fund with Calvert Foundation and are therefore, non-refundable. Donations are on behalf of the Leadership Garden Fund.**
- Eligibility for participation in the randomly selected screening committee to choose quarterly grant awards.
- An additional 11% discount on products and services. Ask about quantity discounts for 50 or more items.

Patron Donor Membership Fee: $250 *minimum*

**Grant Administration:

The Leadership Garden Fund is administered by the Calvert Giving Fund: The Socially Responsible Donor Fund™ of the Calvert Social Investment Foundation on behalf of the owner of Leadership Garden Enterprises, LLC.

Patron Donor Membership Fees (minimum $250) are made payable by check to: **Calvert Foundation** on behalf of the Leadership Garden Fund. Checks are mailed directly to:

Calvert Foundation
PO Box 30084
Bethesda, MD 20824-9948

As the Administrator of the Fund the Calvert Foundation retains the right of final approval of all grant recommendations to ensure compliance with all state and federal laws governing foundation operation and charitable giving.

To learn more about our chosen Fund administrator and social investment funds, visit: *www.calvertgiving.org*

Leadership Garden Enterprises, LLC reserves the right to reject membership of individuals, groups, organizations, and businesses whose mission is not consistent with the principles and practices of growing thriving Leadership Gardens.

Leadership Garden Fund

Cultivation Grants:

The Leadership Garden Fund makes grants available to organizations for the development of leader-friendly gardening "Practice Projects" in the following categories:

- Inclusion projects—Be nonjudgmental
- Safe and Healthy Community projects—Do not enable
- Compassion projects—Use empathy
- Kindness projects—Prune Gossip
- Accountability projects—Eliminate blame
- Healing projects—Eradicate Victimization

Who is eligible?

Members of the Leadership Garden Registry that are charitable organizations and are tax-exempt under IRS Section 501(c)(3) and are public charities under Code Section 609(a), including public universities and educational non-profits.

Size of the grants: $250–$500

Number of Grants and Award Cycles:

One award per cycle representing the six leader-friendly gardening practice categories and all grants are made subject to availability of funds.

ABOUT THE AUTHOR

Debra Slover graduated from Oregon State University with a degree in Health Education. She began her career as a high school teacher and later served as Director of Oregon Student Safety On the Move (OSSOM) for more than twenty years.

Debra is passionate about the possibilities available to youth and adults when given the recognition, skills, and opportunity to express their unique leadership with a purpose and aim.

She founded Synergy in Motion in 2003 to bring vision, relationship, creativity, and a sense of playfulness to leadership.

Debra created the Leadership Garden Legacy in 2006, when she wrote and published *U.N.I.Q.U.E.: Growing the Leader Within.* During the writing of the book, her passion led her. She followed along with Hugh on a personal journey to heal the pain buried deep inside from the loss of her mother, to suicide, when she was just 23. She likened this unexpected detour as her own journey "back to the future" to finally free her own thriving leadership spirit.

As a result, her previous company grew into Leadership Garden Enterprises, LLC in 2007, in order to focus her work to achieve the goal to seed and nurture 11 million Leadership Gardens by 11/11/11. Debra's intent is to inform, empower, and engage the thriving leader within everyone she meets.

She blends more than 30 years of professional experience training, empowering, and serving more than 40,000 youth and adult leaders with a personal touch. During her previous career, she coordinated youth-led statewide conferences, leadership camps, and national conferences. She has been a presenter at numerous national, statewide, and local conferences and seminars, and has served as President of the National Association of Teen Institutes and Chair of the Oregon Coalition to Reduce Underage Drinking.

Debra is the proud mother and grandmother of five children and five grandchildren. Her greatest joy in life is tending to her blended family Leadership Garden.

She lives in Albany, Oregon with her husband, Terry, and dog Mooko.

Notes

NOTES

NOTES

Quick Order Form

▶ **Leadership Garden Empowerment Products:**

U.N.I.Q.U.E.: Growing the Leader Within

    Book: ___ *Hard Cover @ $26.95 ea.* ___ *Paperback @ $18.95 ea.*

    Audio Book: ___ *CD player version @ $24.95 ea.* ___ *Mp3 player version @ $24.95 ea.*

The Leadership Garden Guidebook: ___ *@ $18.95 ea.*

Plus $4.20 Shipping and Handling for first product,
add $2.00 for each additional product

▶ **Leadership Garden Registry Membership:**

    □ *Individual/Family $30*   □ *Group or Organization $60*

    Business: □ *Under 50 employees: $100*   □ *Over 50 employees $200*

Name _____

Mailing Address _____

City _____ State _____ Zip _____

Phone_____ Fax _____ Email _____

Autographed: □ *Yes* □ *No*   *If yes, for whom* _____

Ordering options:

    Online orders: *www.leadergardenpress.com*

    Fax orders: 541-926-3524

    Telephone orders: call 541-928-2232—Have your credit card ready

    Mail orders: Leader Garden Press, Order Department, P.O. Box 841, Albany, OR 97321

For information about quantity discounts, call, fax, or email:
order@leadergardenpress.com

Payment options:

□ Make check payable to: Leader Garden Press

□ Credit Card: □ Visa □ MasterCard □ AMEX □ Discover

    Card number: _____ *Exp. date* _____

    Name on card: _____

Leadership Garden Enterprises LLC donates 11% of the proceeds on all products and
services to the Leadership Garden Fund to support the Cultivation Grants.
To learn more, visit: www.leadershipgardenlegacy.com

79